Iraq

2003

From the Author

As a former Elementary School Teacher, author, mother of four, grandmother of seven and President of Fun Publishing Company, I felt driven to try to explain to children and young adults what led up to the war with Iraq, as well as some of the main events of the war.

I am well aware that much controversy surrounded this war. My main purpose for writing this book was to provide a slice of history for this generation as well as for future generations of young people.

It is my sincere hope that this book will find its way into schools, libraries and private homes.

It follows my SEPTEMBER 11th, 2001 book for children.

Special thanks to:

All of those who fought in the Iraq, 2003 war

Bonnie Foley–an elementary teacher who offered me many ideas

Martin Fryer–the man who worked magic in putting this book together

Val Gottesman–my illustrator as well as good friend

Dr.'s Sophia and Joe Levinson–for their help and encouragement

Mardee Wachs–a special friend since 2nd grade

After September 11th, 2001,

when TERRORISTS flew two airplanes into the twin towers of the World Trade Center in New York City, the U.S. government declared itself committed to ridding the world of TERRORISM.

The events of September 11th made the U.S. government much more vocal about the fact that there were countries around the world intent on developing weapons of mass destruction. These weapons included nuclear bombs as well as chemical and biological weapons. Some of these countries were protecting TERRORISTS and helping them to do their work.

Iraq was one of these countries.

Iraq is a country on the continent of Asia.

It is surrounded by six other countries:
Turkey, Syria, Jordan, Saudi Arabia, Kuwait, and Iran.
All of these countries have borders that touch Iraq.

Turkey

Syria

TIKRIT

BAGHDAD

Iran

Jordan

IRAQ

Saudi Arabia

Kuwait

5

Events leading up to the war

In 1980, the United States chose to help Iraq in the Iraq-Iran war because the U.S. government was very opposed to the anti-American Iranian theocracy. A theocracy is a government under the immediate direction of God. Saddam Hussein of Iraq wanted to set up a government where the church and state are separated as they are in the United States.

Saudi Arabia and many other middle eastern countries would prefer a government like Iran's. That was the last time the U.S. was on friendly terms with Iraq.

In 1988, Hussein used chemical weapons against his own people in the Kurdish town of Halabjah. This was done to defeat the Kurds, a minority group in Iraq, who were attempting to gain independence.

In 1990, Iraqi forces invaded

the neighboring country of Kuwait, in part, because Kuwait had once been part of Iraq. Another motive for the invasion was to take control of the oil fields there.

In January, 1991, a coalition, or union, of numerous groups was formed. It included the United States and various other countries. The coalition launched OPERATION DESERT STORM in order to free Kuwait. The U.S. president then was the first George Bush. OPERATION DESERT STORM had the blessing of the United Nations.

The U.N., or United Nations, is headquartered in New York City and is a multi-purpose international organization. Its primary purpose is to maintain international security and peace. The Security Council of the United Nations consists of fifteen members–5 permanent members and 10 non-permanent members.

The United Nations Security Council

accepted RESOLUTION 686, which outlined conditions
Iraq needed to meet before a formal cease-fire could be arranged.

The U.N. also passed a resolution urging all nations
to stop trading with Iraq except for food and medical supplies.

The coalition pushed the invading soldiers out of Kuwait,
but the Iraqi people kept Saddam Hussein as their leader.
The U.N. decided not to overthrow the government in Iraq.

On September 7th, 2002,

U.S. President George W. Bush, son of the first George Bush,
met with Tony Blair, Prime Minister of the United Kingdom,
at Camp David in the United States.

The two agreed that Iraq had not complied with the U.N. disarmament
resolutions, since they had not cooperated with U.N. weapons inspectors.

Bush and Blair were convinced that the country had weapons of mass
destruction. They also objected to the brutal suppression of dissent
in Iraq by Saddam Hussein.

The two heads of state became determined that they must disarm
Saddam Hussein, destroy his weapons of mass destruction,
and free the Iraqi people.

On September 8, 2002,

Vice-President Dick Cheney reported that Saddam Hussein was trying to build a nuclear bomb. Cheney warned that the U.S. or one of the countries near Iraq, such as Israel, would likely be the target of such a bomb.

Israel is a small country in the middle east that is on the eastern shore of the Mediterranean Sea. It is next to Jordan, Egypt, Syria, and Lebanon. Israel maintains a strong military and has a long history of conflict with the Arab States.

On September 19, 2002,

President Bush asked Congress for the authority to use all means, including military force, if necessary, to disarm and overthrow Saddam Hussein if he continued to defy United Nations' demands for disarmament.

The House of Representatives voted 296-133 and the Senate 77-23 to authorize President Bush to use military force against Iraq.

On November 8, 2002,

the U.N. Security Council unanimously approved a U.S.-drafted resolution, PROPOSITION 1441. This resolution said that Hussein would face serious consequences if he failed to comply with weapons inspectors.

Iraq had never accounted for the weapons they had in stock after the Gulf War, so the Security Council believed they still possessed such weapons.

The U.N. sent weapons inspectors into Iraq two different times and neither time were they able to unearth any weapons of mass destruction.

On February 4, 2003,

Colin Powell, U.S. Secretary of State, presented evidence to
the United Nations that the government in Iraq continued to present
a very real danger to world peace and security.

France, Germany, and Russia wanted to keep the weapons inspectors
in Iraq for a longer period of time. France said it would veto any
resolution that included military force against Iraq at this time.

The United States & The United Kingdom

tried to persuade the U.N. Security Council to pass a resolution
authorizing armed forces to go into Iraq to search for weapons of
mass destruction. The proposed resolution failed.

On March 16, 2003, President Bush met with Prime Minister Tony
Blair and the Spanish Prime Minister José Aznar. The primary issue
they tackled was what to do since diplomacy had apparently failed
in the U.N. Security Council.

Together, they decided it was necessary to proceed with the military
invasion of Iraq. They felt that since the U.N. Security Council had
approved PROPOSITION 1441 in November of 2002, that they had
all the approval they needed to attack Iraq.

A new coalition was formed

of nations that felt strongly that Saddam Hussein had not complied
with weapon inspections and that the time had come to take action.

On March 17, 2003, the U.S. and the United Kingdom realized
that the U.N. Security Council would not approve their
pending resolution to use armed forces in Iraq. Consequently,
they withdrew their resolution and decided to forge ahead
without the support of the U.N. Security Council.

This action,

taken without the blessing of the U.N. Security Council,
caused much dissent around the world.

The newly-formed coalition, under the leadership of President Bush,
gave Saddam Hussein 48 hours to leave Iraq.

President Bush did this because

he and the coalition felt certain that Saddam Hussein
and his family were the main cause of the threat to peace in Iraq.
President Bush delivered a prime time speech to prepare the U.S.
for war. However, despite the deadline, Saddam and his family
refused to leave the country.

THE WAR

By March 19, 2003, more than 35 countries had joined the new coalition. The United States, Great Britain, and Australia sent ground troops from Kuwait City into southern Iraq.

Heading up the entire military operation was General Tommy Franks, who operated from Kuwait City. Donald Rumsfield, the U.S. Secretary of Defense, stayed in the U.S. during the war.

Many of the countries that joined the coalition helped in different ways. Some sent materials needed by the soldiers and ground forces. Others helped by providing intelligence and money. Some promised aid when the rebuilding of Iraq began.

The assault by our troops was massive

in an effort aimed at producing "shock and awe" in the Iraqi troops. It was hoped that the coalition would demonstrate so much force that the Iraqi soldiers would retreat and refuse to fight.

On the first day, bombs and missiles struck more than 1200 targets. Many of these targets were selected by the coalition special forces in advance. These forces are highly trained individuals who enter an area before a mission and pinpoint various targets.

Several things happened during this war

that had not happened in any war previously. The coalition placed EMBEDDED JOURNALISTS, mostly writers and T.V. announcers, in the tanks and trucks.

This procedure allowed these journalists to report almost instantly exactly what was happening each day. This kept T.V. viewers at home up-to-date on what was occurring.

Another first for this war was the use of
PRECISION BOMBING. This type of bombing allowed
the coalition pilots to hit the exact target they desired. In the past,
pilots were only able to hit near the target—often missing it.

Saddam attempted to interfere with this "precision bombing"
by setting some of his oil fields on fire.

Due to PRECISION BOMBING, many of Iraq's public facilities
were able to be saved. This included bridges, electricity grids,
water supplies, schools and hospitals.

The accuracy of bombers was not only new in warfare,
but also gave a great advantage to the coalition,
which would be responsible for rebuilding after the war was over.

After the British troops secured the city of Basra, the U.S. Marines moved into Baghdad, which is Iraq's largest city and its capital.

Many coalition forces thought that the assault on Baghdad would be a giant battle with chemical and biological weapons being used against them. However, while there was some gunfire and resistance, the coalition secured the city even sooner than they had expected.

This was a happy surprise for the Marines, who couldn't believe their good fortune. All of the troops that followed felt the same way.

One important memory

for many people around the world who were watching the war on T.V.
was when, in Baghdad, the Iraqi people, with the help of U.S. Marines,
tore down a large statue of Saddam Hussein. The Iraqi people cheered
and hit the statue with the soles of their shoes.
This is a custom used to show great disgust.

This scene showed the joy of the Iraqi people at being liberated
from their cruel dictator, Saddam Hussein.

After Baghdad was captured,

the next large battle was for Tikrit, Saddam Hussein's hometown. More than 3,000 Marines fought their way into that city. It was the last large city to be taken, thus ending the coalition's large scale action.

AFTER THE FIGHTING,

on April 15, 2003, a group of Iraqi leaders met with representatives from the coalition to discuss the formation of a new government. This group agreed that the rule of law must be paramount. All agreed that Hussein's BAATH PARTY must be dissolved and its effects on Iraqi society must be eliminated. A thirteen-point statement was released after the session.

On May 1, 2003,

President Bush declared an end to major combat in Iraq.
With the outstanding effort of the United States, the United
Kingdom, Australia, Spain and many other coalition countries,
the Iraqi people could now live in a democracy without being
afraid of Saddam Hussein.

History will show us how this war will be judged. Time will tell
whether the weapons of mass destruction will be found.